ıl

THE W.
ANIMAL STORIES

Also in this series

The Walker Book of Funny Stories
The Walker Book of Magical Stories
The Walker Book of Stories for 5+ Year Olds
The Walker Book of Stories for 6+ Year Olds

This collection first published 1995 as
A Walker Treasury: Animal Stories by Walker Books Ltd
87 Vauxhall Walk, London SE11 5HJ

This edition published 2000

2 4 6 8 10 9 7 5 3 1

This book has been typeset in ITC Garamond.

Printed and bound in Great Britain
by The Guernsey Press Co. Ltd

British Library Cataloguing in Publication Data
A catalogue record for this book is
available from the British Library.

ISBN 0-7445-7767-5

The
Walker Book of

animal stories

WALKER BOOKS
AND SUBSIDIARIES
LONDON • BOSTON • SYDNEY

CONTENTS

Joshua

by BERLIE DOHERTY
illustrated by KIM LEWIS

This is the story of a little girl called Willa, who has a friend called Old Miss Annie. She has another friend called Joshua. But it wasn't always like this. When Willa first met Old Miss Annie she was afraid of her. And when she first met Joshua she thought he was a ghost.

Willa was afraid of Old Miss Annie because her hair was like wool and because her voice was full of tiny words. The words were so tiny that they were hardly there at all. They were like secrets. And her hands were full of bumps. Have you ever seen a twig that is all bent and twisted and full of bumps? If you have, then you will know what Old Miss Annie's hands were like. That was why Willa was afraid of her.

And Willa thought Joshua was a ghost because she saw him in Miss Annie's garden in the dark. The sky was full of stars and the moon looked like a boat that night. There was something white in Miss Annie's garden and it seemed to be dancing. That was why Willa thought that Joshua was a ghost. And in the night Joshua cried, and Willa thought it was a ghost crying.

So this is the story of how Willa met Old Miss Annie and became her friend. But first she had to say goodbye to Rose.

Willa says goodbye to Rose

Mum and Dad had bought a house in a big town, far away. They would have to drive all day to get to the new house, and when they got there they would be in another country. They would cross over many rivers and drive along many roads. The sky would turn black and all the stars would come out before they reached the house in the town where Willa was going to live.

But first she had to say goodbye to Rose. Rose came upstairs to her room with her. They packed all Willa's toys in a big trunk.

"It looks like a box of treasures," said Rose.

"It is," said Willa.

She put a Bear called Billy on the top of all the

toys and closed the lid of the trunk. The removal men carried it downstairs to the van that would take it to Willa's new house. There was no bed in the room because that was already in the removal van, so Rose and Willa sat on the floor and held hands. They cried because they would never see each other again.

When they went downstairs they felt shy of each other. Willa followed Mum and Dad to the car and she didn't know what to say to Rose. It was as if they had never been friends at all. But when they were driving to the new house, over all the rivers and through all the strange cities, Willa kept thinking about Rose. The sky turned black and all the stars came out. They reached another country.

Willa knew then that she would never have another friend like Rose again. And it was true.

By the time they arrived at the new house Willa was fast asleep. Mum carried her up to her new bedroom and put her in her own bed. Dad carried up the trunk. He opened it and looked at all the toys that were like treasures. Then he picked out a Bear called Billy and put him on Willa's pillow.

When Willa woke up she didn't know where she was. The ceiling was too high. The window was too far away. The walls had flowers on instead of clowns. Then she found a Bear called Billy on her pillow and she hugged him. She remembered that she would never see Rose again and she began to cry. Outside in a garden she heard something else crying. It sounded like a little, lost, ghosty child.

Willa looks for a friend

Mum and Dad and Willa were busy all day, unpacking boxes and sorting things out.

"We'll paint all the doors and paper all the walls," said Dad. "And you can choose the colours for your room, Willa."

"It'll soon look like home," Mum told her.

But Willa knew it would never look like home. That afternoon she went with Mum to the shops at the top of the road.

"We'll see if we can find some friends for you," Mum said.

But they looked in every front garden that they passed, and there was no sign anywhere of any children for Willa to play with.

"Don't worry," Mum said. "You'll soon make friends when you start at the school."

"I don't want a friend," said Willa.

She only wanted one friend, and that was Rose, who lived in another country far away over all the rivers.

That night Willa hugged a Bear called Billy, and listened to the sound of sad, ghostly crying in somebody's garden.

Old Miss Annie

Next day Willa met Old Miss Annie for the very first time. She was afraid of her. She heard a knock at the door, and saw Mum bringing an old lady into the kitchen. The lady had hair like wool. Willa had never seen hair like that before. And when the old lady spoke, her voice was full of tiny words. They were so tiny that you could hardly hear them. They were more like secrets. Willa put her hands over her ears so she couldn't hear the tiny voice.

Old Miss Annie sat down on the new kitchen chair and peered at Willa as if she couldn't quite see her.

"Would you like a cup of tea, Miss Annie?" Mum said.

"I would," said Miss Annie, in her tiny voice.

That was when Willa saw Miss Annie's hands. They were full of bumps, like a twig that's all bent and twisted. Willa closed her eyes so she couldn't see them. And that was when Miss Annie told Willa one of her secrets. The words were so tiny that Willa could hardly hear them, but what she thought Miss Annie said was:

"Do you know what I've got in my garden? A ghost!"

The ghost in the garden

That night when Willa was in bed she heard the sound of crying in someone's garden. It was such a sad, lost, lonely cry. She and a Bear called Billy climbed out of bed to have a look through the window. The sky was full of stars, and the moon was like a boat that night. And in one of the gardens she saw a white shape. Willa clutched a Bear called Billy.

"It's the ghost!" she whispered.

Then the white shape began to move, just as if it were dancing.

"Look at the ghost dancing!" whispered Willa.

And then it began to cry, such a sad, lonely, ghosty cry.

"It's the ghost crying," said Willa. "Poor ghost!"

Every night Willa looked out of her window and saw the white shape dancing, and every night she heard its sad, lost, lonely, ghosty cry.

One day, when she was going to the shops with Mum, they saw Old Miss Annie coming out of her front door. She came slowly down towards them, peering at them as though she couldn't quite see them. When she remembered who they were, she smiled. Willa held Mum's hand tightly.

"How do you like your new house?" Old Miss Annie asked Mum. Her voice was so tiny that it was hardly there at all.

"It's lovely," Mum said. "But I wish we could find a friend for Willa."

Willa thought about Rose, who lived far away in another country. She knew she would never see Rose again. She closed her eyes and tried to pretend that it didn't matter. Then Old Miss Annie bent towards her and told her another of her secrets.

"I want you to come and see Joshua," she whispered.

Willa opened her eyes. She held Mum's hand tighter than ever because she was so afraid of Old Miss Annie, but she asked the question that she wanted to ask.

"Does Joshua live in your garden?" she asked.

Old Miss Annie nodded.

Willa still held Mum's hand tightly.

14

"I've seen him dancing," she said.

Old Miss Annie nodded again. Willa saw how pale and smiling her eyes were.

"I've heard him crying in the night," Willa said.

And then she saw how Old Miss Annie's eyes turned sad.

"I think he's lonely," Old Miss Annie said, and the words were so tiny that they were more like secrets that had never been told to anyone else before.

Old Miss Annie held out her hand. It was full of bumps, just like a twig that's all twisted. Even though Willa was afraid of Old Miss Annie she liked the way her eyes looked sad and smiling at the same time.

"You go and see Joshua," said Mum. "And I'll call for you when I come back from the shops."

So Willa let go of Mum's hand and followed Old Miss Annie up her path and round to the garden at the back. And that was how she met Joshua.

Joshua the ghost

Joshua had yellow eyes and a beard like white silk. He had horns that twisted round themselves, and a big mouth like a saucer. He was tied by a rope to a post under the trees in Miss Annie's little garden, and when he tried to move away from it he jumped in the

air. It was just as if he were dancing. And then he gave his sad cry, and Willa felt as if she were crying too.

"Poor ghost," she said.

Old Miss Annie went over to Joshua and patted him, and slipped the rope off the stick. "I'll move the tether-pin," she said. "Then he can have some fresh grass."

"Why is he tied up?" asked Willa.

"Because he'd eat everything in my garden," Old Miss Annie chuckled. "And he'd have hiccups."

Joshua cried again, and Willa put her hands over her ears.

"Why does he cry so much?" she shouted.

"I think he's lonely," Old Miss Annie said. "And this garden is too small for him."

Willa thought that Joshua didn't look like a ghost at all. He looked like a small white horse, or a big white dog, or a sheep. "He doesn't look like a ghost," she said.

Old Miss Annie put her head a little to one side as if she couldn't hear Willa properly.

"We could take him for a walk, if you like," she said.

They both had to hold on to Joshua's rope. He

skipped in front of them, tucking his head down and kicking his legs out. Willa and Old Miss Annie hung on to his rope and laughed all the way up the road. His feet made little scratching noises on the pavement. Everyone they passed smiled at them and said, "Hello, Miss Annie," and "Hello, Joshua," and when Old Miss Annie introduced them to Willa they said, "Hello, Willa," too, and smiled. Some of them were children.

Willa felt proud to be the one taking Joshua for a walk.

When they got back to Old Miss Annie's house they were both out of breath with running behind Joshua. They put him back in the garden, and that was when Miss Annie told Willa the story of how Joshua came to stay with her.

"One day," Old Miss Annie said, "I saw a picture of Joshua in the paper. I fell in love with him! And under the picture it said:

HOME WANTED FOR JOSHUA
If no home is found for him, he must die.

"I was so sorry for him that I phoned up and Joshua came to stay. I do love him!" Her eyes sparkled. "But he's lonely, isn't he, Willa?"

Willa nodded.

"He cries all night," said Old Miss Annie.

Willa nodded again. "He needs a friend," she said.

Joshua's new friend

That night Willa told Dad about Joshua. "He needs to be in a field full of ghosts," she said.

"I'll see if I can find one," Dad smiled.

And he did. He put Joshua in the back of his van, and Old Miss Annie and Willa stroked him all the way to the countryside. They drove past a dark wood and over a bridge and came at last to the farm that belonged to Dad's friend Alison. The farm had a field with three horses in it and another field with goats.

Alison opened the gate to the field that was full of goats and Joshua danced into it, and all the other goats danced down to Joshua like friends.

"You'll come and see him soon, won't you?" Alison said as she waved goodbye to them.

"Joshua's a goat really, isn't he?" said Willa.

Old Miss Annie looked at her and nodded. She put out her hand, that was full of bumps like an old bent twig, and Willa held it tight.

Little Ivan

by VIVIAN FRENCH
illustrated by CHRIS FISHER

In the middle of the world there was a forest of tall
pine trees, and in among the pine trees was a
wooden house. Little Ivan and his grandmother
lived in the house, and very happy they were. Every
day Grandmother went to work in the village
beyond the forest, and before she went she would
cook Little Ivan his dinner and leave it in the oven to
keep warm.

"Now, Little Ivan, when are you to eat your
dinner?"

"At twelve o'clock, Grandmother, and not before."

"You remember that, Little Ivan."

"I will, Grandmother, I will."

And Grandmother would set off on her long walk
through the trees to the village. In the evening when
she came home she and Little Ivan would eat their
supper, and then if it was light they would walk

under the trees and collect fir-cones. If it was dark they would sit in front of the fire and tell each other stories.

One morning Grandmother cooked Little Ivan a bowl of bacon and red beans, and put it in the oven to keep warm.

"Now, Little Ivan, when are you to eat your dinner?"

"At twelve o'clock, Grandmother, and not before."

"You remember that, Little Ivan."

"I will, Grandmother, I will."

And Grandmother put on her shawl and set off on her long walk through the trees. She hadn't gone very far when she heard singing – a wild singing that she hadn't heard in the woods for a long, long time. Grandmother stopped and listened.

"Yoi! Yoi! Yoi!"

"Well!" said Grandmother to herself. "If I'm not much mistaken, that there is Old Mother Wolf, and if Old Mother Wolf is singing that song she's got wolf-cubs with her. And if she and her cubs have come to live in our forest then that means *trouble*. I'd better hurry home and tell Little Ivan." And Grandmother turned around and went hurrying back along the path to the wooden house.

Little Ivan was very surprised to see Grandmother coming back. "Whatever is it?" he asked.

Grandmother was wheezing and panting.

"Little Ivan," she puffed, "if I'm not much mistaken Old Mother Wolf has come to live in our forest. And if Old Mother Wolf is here with her wolf-cubs then that means *trouble,* so you be sure and keep the door and the windows *tight shut*!"

"Yes, Grandmother," said Little Ivan.

"You remember that, Little Ivan."

"I will, Grandmother, I will."

And Grandmother turned herself around again and went hurrying back along the path.

Little Ivan went back to playing with his fir-cones. His bowl of bacon and red beans was in the oven, and the smell came out of the oven and into the kitchen where Little Ivan was playing.

Mmmmm … that smells very good, thought Little Ivan.

The smell came out of the kitchen and into the house, and out of the house and into the forest. It floated away in and out of the tall pine trees until it reached the very darkest part of the forest, and there it drifted down into a deep dark cave. Inside the cave

was Mother Wolf and her three little wolf-cubs, and they all sat up and sniffed.

"Yip, yip, yip!" snapped the three little wolf-cubs. "That smells *very* good!"

"Yoi, yoi, yoi," said Mother Wolf. "It smells *very* good indeed. Shall I fetch it for you for your dinner?"

"Yes-ess-ess!" The three little wolf-cubs rubbed their tummies and rolled over and over.

"I'll be off then," said Mother Wolf, and she began running through the woods on her sneaky soft pitter-patter feet.

In and out of the tall trees she ran, until she came to Little Ivan's house, and when she reached the door she knocked three times.

"Who's that?" said Little Ivan, and he ran to the window.

Mother Wolf leaped in the air and ran right around the house. She ran so fast that her ears blew back, and her whiskers whistled in the wind, and as she ran she called out,

"Open the door just a crack, just a crack,
And I'll give you a ride on my back."

I'd *love* to go as fast as that, thought Little Ivan, and

he opened the door just as wide as a crack.

CRASH! Before Little Ivan had time to say hello or goodbye, Mother Wolf was in the house and running up and down the stairs. Into the kitchen she rushed, and she snatched the bowl of bacon and red beans from the oven. Then with a leap and a bound she was out of the door, and Little Ivan could only see the trees waving where she had dashed past. On and on through the trees she ran, until she saw the three little wolf-cubs sitting up and waiting for her.

"Here, my dears," she said. "Eat up and be glad."

And the three little wolf-cubs ate up all the bacon and red beans, and they licked their lips and they rubbed their tummies.

"Yummyummyumm," they said.

When Grandmother came home that evening Little Ivan was waiting at the door.

"Well, Little Ivan, did you enjoy your dinner today?"

Little Ivan shook his head.

"Why ever not?" Grandmother stared at him. "You're not going to tell me that you let Old Mother Wolf into the house?"

Little Ivan nodded miserably.

"*Well!* Don't you go expecting me to be sorry for you! Now tomorrow, you be sure and keep that door tightly *shut*!"

Little Ivan nodded again. "Oh, yes, Grandmother."

"T'ch, t'ch, t'ch," said Grandmother crossly, and she began to make their supper.

The next morning Grandmother cooked Little Ivan chicken and barley for his dinner, and she put the bowl in the oven to keep warm.

"Now, Little Ivan, when are you to eat your dinner?"

"At twelve o'clock, Grandmother, and not before."

"And what will you do with the door, Little Ivan?"

"Keep it tight shut, Grandmother."

"You remember that, Little Ivan."

"I will, Grandmother, I will."

And Grandmother put on her shawl and set off on her long walk through the trees. Little Ivan sat down to play with his fir-cones. The smell of the chicken and barley was already creeping out of the oven and into the kitchen, and Little Ivan nodded.

"That will taste very good at twelve o'clock."

The smell came out of the kitchen and into the house, and out of the house and into the forest. It floated away in and out of the tall pine trees until it reached the very darkest part of the forest, and there it drifted down into Mother Wolf's cave. The three little wolf-cubs jumped in the air.

"Yip, yip, yip! That smells even better than yesterday!"

"Yoi, yoi, yoi," said Mother Wolf. "It does indeed. Shall I fetch it for you for your dinner?"

"Yes-ess-ess!" The three little wolf-cubs rubbed their tummies and skipped up and down.

"I'll be off then," said Mother Wolf, and she began running through the woods on her sneaky soft pitter-patter feet.

In and out of the tall trees she ran, until she came to Little Ivan's house, and when she reached the door she knocked three times.

"Who's that?" said Little Ivan, and he ran to the window to look out.

Mother Wolf leapt in the air and ran right around the house and right around again. She ran so fast that her ears blew back, and her whiskers whistled in the wind, and as she ran she called out,

"Open the window a crack, just a crack,
And I'll give you a ride on my back."

I'd *love* to go as fast as that, thought Little Ivan, and he opened the window just as wide as a crack.

CRASH! Before Little Ivan had time to say please or thank you, Mother Wolf was in the house and running up and down the stairs. Into the kitchen she rushed, and snatched the bowl of chicken and barley from the oven. Then with a leap and a bound she was out of the door, and Little Ivan could only see the trees waving where she had dashed past. On and on through the trees she went, until she saw the three little wolf-cubs sitting up and waiting for her.

"Here, my dears," she said. "Eat up and be glad."

And the three little wolf-cubs ate up all the chicken and barley, and they licked their lips and rubbed their tummies.

"Yummyummyumm," they said.

When Grandmother came home that evening Little Ivan was standing by the window.

"Well, Little Ivan, did you enjoy your dinner today?"

Little Ivan shook his head.

"Oh, Little Ivan! You *didn't* let Old Mother Wolf into the house again?"

Little Ivan nodded miserably.

"Well!" Grandmother sat down on a chair with a flump. "Don't you go expecting me to be sorry for you! And don't go expecting any dinner tomorrow, either. I don't cook nice dinners for you to give to that old wolf and her family. You'll have bread and water tomorrow, and be thankful."

"Yes, Grandmother," said Little Ivan.

The next morning Grandmother got up later than usual. She cut Little Ivan a thick slice of bread and poured him out a glass of water, and then she locked the rest of the bread in the cupboard.

"There's your dinner, Little Ivan," she said. "And when are you to eat it?"

"At twelve o'clock, Grandmother."

"You remember that, Little Ivan, and mind that you eat it yourself."

"I will, Grandmother. I will."

And Grandmother put on her shawl and set off on her long walk through the trees. Little Ivan went slowly down to the kitchen, and looked sadly at the empty oven.

No good dinner today, he thought, and picked up his fir-cones.

Mother Wolf and her three little wolf-cubs were

sitting outside their cave sniffing the air.

"Where's our dinner, Mother?" asked the cubs.

Mother Wolf shook her head. "No dinner today, my dears."

"Ow, ow, ow!" howled the little wolf-cubs. "No dinner today!"

Mother Wolf sniffed the air again. "Perhaps Little Ivan has a cold dinner today? Cheese? A ham? A sausage?"

"Yip, yip, yip!" snapped the three little wolf-cubs. "Go and see, dear Mother, go and see."

"I'll be off, then," said Mother Wolf, and she began running through the woods on her sneaky soft pitter-patter feet.

In and out of the tall trees she ran, until she came to Little Ivan's house, and when she reached the door she knocked three times.

"That's Mother Wolf!" said Little Ivan, and he ran into the kitchen. Quickly, quickly he ate his bread, and quickly, quickly he drank his water.

"There! Now I've eaten my dinner!" he said, and he hurried to the window.

Mother Wolf leapt in the air and ran right around the house three times. She ran so fast that her ears blew back and her whiskers whistled in the wind,

and as she ran she called out,

*"Open the door or the window a crack,
And I'll give you a ride on my back."*

Oh, how I'd *love* to go as fast as that, thought Little Ivan, and he flung open the window as wide as it would go.

WHOOSH! Mother Wolf leapt into the house, and ran up and down the stairs. Into the kitchen she rushed, but there she stopped. There was nothing in the oven, and nothing on the shelf.

"I've eaten my dinner!" Little Ivan shouted. "Now give me my ride!"

Mother Wolf stood very still. "Climb on to my back, Little Ivan," she said, "and hold on!"

Little Ivan climbed on to Mother Wolf's back, and with a leap and a bound she was out of the window. Little Ivan held on tightly to her rough tough fur. They were going so fast that the trees were a green blur on either side of them, and Little Ivan's hair streamed behind him. He was so happy that he laughed and sang, and the wind carried his song far away beyond the trees.

"Oh!" Little Ivan gasped as Mother Wolf carried

him right into the middle of her dark, cold cave.

"Ow!" said Little Ivan as the three little wolf-cubs pulled his hair and bit his fingers and scratched his feet.

"No dinner today, my dears," said Mother Wolf, "but I've brought you something to play with. It's too thin to eat, but we'll keep it to sweep and to dust and to clean. Won't that be nice?"

"Yes-ess-ess!" said the cubs, and they rolled Little Ivan over and over until he was dusty and dirty and very unhappy indeed.

Grandmother saw the wide open window when she was still a long way away. "Oh dear, oh dear, oh dear!" she said, and hurried up the path. "Little Ivan! Where are you?"

There was no answer. Grandmother called again, but all that she could hear was the wind hushing the trees.

"I do believe that Old Mother Wolf has taken my Little Ivan away," Grandmother said at last. "Oh dearie, dearie me – whatever shall I do?" And she began puffing and panting back the way she had come.

When she reached the village, she saw the

children's band marching round and round the village square. "Tantantara! Boom boom boom! Squeak eek tiddle squeak eek!" When the children saw Grandmother hurrying down the path towards them they stopped at once and ran to meet her.

"What is it, Grandmother? Don't cry, we'll help you!" Grandmother wiped her eyes.

"It's Old Mother Wolf," she said. "I think she's taken my Little Ivan, and I don't know what to do."

"We'll fetch him back," said one of the children. "We'll blow our trumpets!"

"And bang our drums!"

"And play our violins!"

"We'll play Old Mother Wolf the loudest tune she's ever heard!"

Grandmother blew her nose, and began to smile. "You've given me such an idea. I know *just* what to do now. Shall we be off?"

"Yes, yes, yes!" shouted all the children.

"Shhhh!" said Grandmother. "We must be very quiet."

"Shhhh!" said all the children, and they began to tiptoe in and out of the tall pine trees under the light of the moon.

The forest was very dark all around Mother Wolf's

home. The children followed Grandmother until they all stood in a line outside the deep dark cave, and they watched and they listened.

"Zzzzzzz zzzzzzz zzzzzzz."

"I think Old Mother Wolf is asleep," whispered Grandmother. "Are the trumpeters ready?"

"Yes, Grandmother," whispered the children.

"One, two, three – PLAY!"

"Tantara! Tantara! Tantara!" went the trumpets.

Down at the bottom of the cave Mother Wolf and the wolf-cubs and Little Ivan woke up with a start.

"What a horrible noise!" said Mother Wolf crossly. "Little wolf-cub, tell them to go away!"

The first little wolf-cub ran up to the top of the cave. "Please go away," he said. But before he could say anything more, Grandmother snatched him up and wrapped him tightly in her shawl.

"That's one," she whispered. "Are the drummers ready?"

"Ready, Grandmother," whispered the children.

"One, two, three – PLAY!"

"Boom! Boom! Boom!" went the drums.

Down at the bottom of the cave Mother Wolf shook her head.

"That's even louder than last time," she said. "Little

wolf-cub, tell them to go away."

The second little wolf-cub ran up to the top of the cave. "Go away," she said, but before she could say anything more, Grandmother snatched her up and wrapped her tightly in her shawl.

"That's two," whispered Grandmother. "Are the violins ready?"

"Ready, Grandmother," whispered the children.

"One, two, three – PLAY!"

"Squeak eek tiddle squeak eek!" went the violins.

Down at the bottom of the cave Mother Wolf was growing angry.

"That's a terrible noise," she said. "How can I sleep with a noise like that going on? Little wolf-cub, go and tell them that if they don't go away *at once* I will come and eat them all up."

The third little wolf-cub ran up to the top of the cave, and looked around at Grandmother and all the children.

"If you don't go away *at once*," he said, "Mother Wolf will eat you all up!"

"Oh, she will, will she?" said Grandmother, and she snatched up the little wolf-cub and wrapped him up in her shawl with his brother and sister.

"That's three!" said Grandmother. "Now, is

everybody ready?"

"Ready!" said the children.

"One, two, three – PLAY!" said Grandmother. And all the children began to play together.

"Tantara! Boom! Squeak eek tiddle!"

Down at the bottom of the cave Mother Wolf was very angry indeed.

"This is *too much*!" she said, and she rushed up to the top of the cave with her sharp white teeth shining in the moonlight.

"If you don't go away," she snarled, "I shall eat you all up from the tops of your heads to the tips of your toes!"

"Just one minute, Mother Wolf," said Grandmother. "Let me tell you that I've caught your three little wolf-cubs, and I'm not giving them back until I have my Little Ivan safe and sound."

"Mother! Mother! Mother!" called the three little wolf-cubs bundled up in Grandmother's shawl.

Mother Wolf sat down in front of her cave and scratched her ear.

"Very well," she said. "He's too thin for a dinner." And she turned round and went down into the cave.

A moment later Little Ivan came crawling out. He was dusty and dirty and scratched and bitten, but when he saw Grandmother he shouted, "GRANDMOTHER!"

"LITTLE IVAN!" shouted Grandmother, and they hugged each other as hard as they could while all the children cheered.

"Now," Grandmother said, "let's see about these little wolf-cubs." She unwrapped them all from her shawl, and they ran to Mother Wolf.

"We want our dinners!" they cried. "We're hungry!"

"Shall we go over the hills and far away?" said Mother Wolf.

"Yes-ess-ess!" said the three little wolf-cubs, and they and Mother Wolf ran away, in and out of the tall trees and out of the forest and over the hills on their sneaky soft pitter-patter feet while above them the moon shone down.

"Well!" said Grandmother. "That's well gone! And now let's all go home."

"Hurrah!" shouted all the children. And they held Little Ivan's hands and ran with him through the trees to the wooden house.

Grandmother made them all

a fine feast, and when they had eaten as much as they could, they sat down and told stories of woods and wolves and forests and fir-cones. And the next morning when Grandmother went down the path to work she took Little Ivan with her, and he went to school with all the other children, so if ever Old Mother Wolf came to sing her songs again in the forest of tall pine trees in the middle of the world there would be nobody there to hear her.

Tod and the Desperate Search

by PHILIPPA PEARCE
illustrated by ADRIANO GON

The next-door neighbour, old Mr Parkin, was going away for a week's holiday. But what was going to happen to his cat, Ginger, while he was away?

"Can't Mr Parkin take Ginger on holiday with him?" asked Tod. "Wouldn't Ginger like a holiday?"

"Cats like staying at home," said Tod's mother. "Your dad and I have offered to feed Ginger while Mr Parkin's away;

and Mr Parkin has said, Yes, please. He's given me his back-door key, so that we can go into the house and get the cat food every day. Ginger has half a tin of cat food every morning and another half tin every evening."

"My, that's a lot for a cat!" said Tod's father.

"Ginger's a big cat," said Tod's mother.

Tod said, "Can I come with you when you go to feed Ginger?"

"Of course," said his mother; and his father said, "You could be a great help, Tod."

So it was settled.

Ginger was a big cat, yellowy brown all over except for one white front leg. He was rather a silent cat. He never miaowed; but he purred when he was tickled behind his ear. He liked to be out of doors most of the time.

On the first morning after old Mr Parkin had gone on holiday, Tod was at home with his father. They took Mr Parkin's key and went round to the back of his house. There was Ginger at the back door, his tail waving high in the air, ready for his breakfast. They unlocked the door and went into Mr Parkin's kitchen, Ginger slipping in ahead of them. Mr Parkin had left his kitchen very

neat and clean; and the door between the kitchen and the rest of the house was shut. This was so that Ginger could not go wandering off through the other rooms.

Tod's father opened a tin of cat food, while Tod washed the cat dish that Ginger had eaten his supper from the evening before. Ginger had two cat dishes to eat from, one being used, one being washed. So he always had a clean dish for his food.

Tod's father put down the clean dish with half a tin of cat food in it. Ginger began eating very fast.

While Ginger ate, Tod's father put the half-used tin into the fridge; and Tod fetched Ginger's water bowl that always stood just outside the back door. He emptied the old water away and refilled the bowl with clean, fresh water from the tap and put the bowl outside again.

By now Ginger had finished his breakfast and he walked out into the garden again, very pleased with himself. He settled on the lawn in a patch of sunshine and began cleaning his fur.

"But where will he sleep tonight?" asked Tod.

"If it's cold," said Tod's father, "he can get

through the cat door into the boiler-house. It's always warm in there, and Mr Parkin has put a basket there with an old blanket in it. But if the night's not cold, then Ginger will probably sleep out in the garden under a bush."

Tod's father locked Mr Parkin's back door again. They said goodbye to Ginger and went back to their own house.

That evening Tod didn't go with his mother – it was her turn – to give Ginger his supper, because he was being bathed and put to bed by his father. But every morning Tod went with his mother or his father to give Ginger his breakfast, wash a cat dish, and renew the water in the drinking bowl.

And every morning there was Ginger at Mr Parkin's back door, tail in the air, eager for his breakfast.

Then one morning, almost at the end of Mr Parkin's week away from home, Tod went as usual with his father, and Ginger was not waiting at Mr Parkin's back door.

"Bother," said Tod's father. "That cat's late for his breakfast." And he began to call him: "Ginger! Ginger!"

No Ginger came.

"You call him, Tod," said his father.

So Tod called him: "Ginger! Ginger!" and then "Ginger-ninger!" and then "Ginger-winger!"

They both called and called, but no cat came. In the end they decided to leave the dish of cat food just outside the back door, with fresh water in the drinking bowl. Perhaps Ginger would come later.

At midday Tod and his father went round to Mr Parkin's back door again. There was the dish of cat food still. It looked as if birds might have pecked at it; but most of the food remained. Ginger would have eaten the whole lot and left the dish clean. So Ginger had not been.

When Tod's mother came home, they told her about Ginger's having gone missing. "What a worry!" she said. "Mr Parkin's back the day after tomorrow. I don't know what he'll say if Ginger's not there to greet him."

"Perhaps the cat's got shut in somewhere," said Tod's father.

"Perhaps in Mr Parkin's house," said Tod.

"No," said his mother. "You remember the door from the kitchen into the rest of the house

53

has always been kept shut. And Mr Parkin told me himself that he shut and locked every window in the house, upstairs and down, before he left."

"There's still his garden shed and his greenhouse and that boiler-house," said Tod's father. "We must search everywhere."

So all three of them went to look in Mr Parkin's garden shed and his greenhouse and the boiler-house. They even came back and looked in their own garden shed.

No Ginger anywhere.

They began to feel desperate.

Tod had never before helped to give Ginger his supper; but today, after his bath, he put on his pyjamas and his dressing-gown and his bedroom slippers and went round with his mother and his father to see if Ginger had turned up for his supper.

He hadn't.

Tod's mother said, "I hope that he hasn't strayed on to the main road and been run over by a car."

"I think Ginger's probably too sensible for that," said Tod's father.

Tod said, "I don't want Ginger to be dead."

His parents comforted him. They mustn't give up hope yet, they said. Who knows? Ginger might still turn up tomorrow.

The next morning, however, at breakfast time, outside Mr Parkin's back door, there was still no Ginger.

"I'm afraid that something must have happened to him," Tod's mother said sadly. And Tod's father said, "Wasn't Mr Parkin going to telephone us this evening, just to confirm that he's coming home tomorrow? What on earth are we going to say to him?"

Tod's mother just said, "Oh dear!"

That morning Tod felt very miserable. His mother was at home, and she suggested various interesting things that he might like to do; but he didn't want to do any of them. He just wandered round the garden, calling, "Ginger-ninger, where are you? Ginger-winger, come home!"

Tod knew that they'd looked into their own garden shed, but he still went there again, because there seemed nowhere else he could look. The first time he looked in, he looked very quickly, because, of course, he really knew that Ginger wasn't there. The second time he decided he must look more thoroughly, all round: at the workbench under the window; at the cupboard at the far end, where his father kept his special tools; at the garden spades and forks and hoes that hung in a row along the remaining wall. Tod even got down on all fours and looked under the lawnmower. No Ginger, of course.

That was the second time that Tod looked into the shed.

The third time he looked in, he was quietly crying to himself. It was getting dark inside the shed. He looked at the cupboard at the far end. At the bottom of the cupboard, the door fitted badly and left a gap. Suddenly, through that gap, came snaking something white – a long white furry arm.

"Ginger!" shouted Tod, and rushed to open the cupboard door; but the cupboard was kept bolted, and the bolt was too high for Tod to reach. So he ran back to the house to fetch his mother, who came hurrying at once. She unbolted the cupboard door and opened it – and out stalked Ginger!

Ginger didn't seem ill or even thin; but he did seem cross. He didn't want to be stroked or even tickled behind his ear. He went straight to the fence that separated the two gardens. He crouched at the bottom of the fence for a moment, and then with a leap he was at the top of the fence, and then over into his own garden – home!

Tod's mother fetched Mr Parkin's key and they went round to his back door. There was Ginger, his tail waving in the air, ready for his food. He had already had a long drink, they could tell, from his bowl of water. They fed him more than half a tin of cat food, as he had missed so many meals. Then they locked up again and went home.

Later, Tod's father heard all about how Tod had found Ginger in the tool cupboard. "What a sly cat!" he said. "Yes, I remember going to that cupboard to get a tool on the very day he disappeared. I left the cupboard door open for just a few minutes while I did something at the workbench. While my back was turned, he must have slipped in."

"Cats are like that," said Tod's mother.

"Anyway," said Tod's father, "we'll have something to tell old Parkin when he rings up."

Tod began jumping with excitement. "When Mr Parkin rings, can I tell him about Ginger? Can I? Can I?"

"Why not?" said his father, and looked at Tod's mother. She said, "I think Tod should tell the whole story. After all, he found Ginger. He is the hero of our desperate search."

Old Greyface

by MICHAEL ROSEN
illustrated by CAROLINE HOLDEN

Once upon a time in China there were three little girls called Seng, Ton and Po Ki. Seng was the oldest. One day their mum said, "I'm going on a long journey to see my mother, your grandmother. I won't get back till tomorrow morning, so Seng, you look

after Ton and Po Ki. Stay in the house and don't let anyone come in."

Outside, Old Greyface, the wolf, watched the girls' mum leave the house. He waited till it got dark and then crept up to the door. Up he got on his back legs and tightened his throat to make his voice sound high. Then he knocked on the door and called out in a squeaky voice, "Open up the door for your poor old granny."

"But Mum's on her way to see *you*," said Seng.

"Oh dear," squeaked Old Greyface, "we must have missed each other on the way. Let me in, girls."

"Your voice sounds a bit funny, Granny," said Seng, but Ton and Po Ki ran and opened the door.

In stepped the wolf and quickly blew out the candle, so the girls couldn't see him.

"Why did you blow out the candle, Granny?" asked Seng.

"The light hurts my eyes," said Old Greyface. Then he lowered himself down on to a chair.

"Ayeeeeee!" he screamed, for he had sat down right on his tail.

"Ayeeeeee!"

"What's the matter, Granny?" asked Seng.

"Oooooh, it's my back," said the wolf. "This chair's not very comfortable for me. I think I'll sit in your basket."

Old Greyface stepped over to the basket and dropped into it, exhausted from all this walking about on his hind legs. But as he dropped down, he let his tail flop into the basket after him – plomph!

"What was that noise?" said Seng.

"What noise?" said Old Greyface.

"That plomph," said Seng.

"Ah yes," said Old Greyface, "that's the chicken I've brought for your mother, dear."

Seng peered through the darkness. This wasn't Granny, she was sure. She thought quickly. Then she said, "Do you like nuts, Granny?"

"Nuts? What nuts?" said Old Greyface.

"Magic Yum-Yum Nuts!" said Seng. "Ooh, they're delicious. If you eat one, you want another. And when you eat another, you want another and another and another."

"Are they nicer to eat than little girls?" said Old Greyface.

"Oh yes, much nicer," said Seng.

"Where are these Magic Yum-Yum Nuts?" said Old Greyface. "I must have some."

"They grow on the tree at the corner of the house. I'll tell you what, Granny, you wait here, and we'll go and get you some of the Magic Yum-Yum Nuts."

"You never told us about them," said Ton.

"Shush!" said Seng. "Just follow me."

When they got outside, Seng said to her sisters, "Listen, it isn't Granny, it's a wolf."

"Oh no, what do we do now?" asked Po Ki.

"Follow me," said Seng, and she climbed up the tree. Ton and Po Ki followed after.

Back in the house, Old Greyface waited and waited. In the end he went out to look for the girls.

"Where are you, girls?" he called out.

"Up here, Granny," said Seng. "These Magic Yum-Yum Nuts are so delicious. They're the sweetest, juiciest things you'll ever taste in all your life."

"Bring them down here," shouted Old Greyface.

"But, Granny," said Seng, "these are *magic* nuts and the moment they leave the tree, they turn into wood. You'll have to come up if you want some, and bite them off the tree like we do."

"Don't tell him to come up here," said Ton, "he'll eat us up."

"Shush!" said Seng.

Poor Old Greyface. He walked and walked round the tree. He didn't know what to do. He couldn't climb trees.

"Your granny's too old to climb the tree," he said. "Show a little respect and kindness to your elders – come down here."

"Oh wait, Granny," said Seng. "I've got an idea. Back in the house, there's a long piece of rope. Bring the rope and the big basket you sat in, and we can pull you up to the top of the tree. Then you'll be able to eat all the Magic Yum-Yum Nuts you like."

By now the wolf was desperate to eat the nuts, or the girls, or both. He ran to the house and rushed back to the tree with the rope and the basket, in a trice. He threw the rope up into the air. The girls caught it, and then he tied the rope to the basket and climbed in.

"Come on, girls, pull me up!" shouted Old Greyface. He was so excited.

Seng pulled and pulled. Up went the basket. Up, up, up, till suddenly – flip! Seng let go of the rope. Down went the wolf and landed on the ground with a great WHAM!

"Oh, I'm sorry, Granny," shouted Seng. "I'm not very strong. Are you all right?"

"Oooh, my head!" said Old Greyface. "Listen, get one of your sisters to help you next time. Now pull me up."

Up, up, up went the basket, even higher this time, then – flip! They let go of the rope and down went the wolf again – WHAM!

"Oh, Granny, I'm so sorry," said Seng. "The rope slipped through our fingers. Are you all right?"

"Oooh, my legs!" said Old Greyface. He was in agony, but now he was even more desperate to get to the girls and the nuts.

"Listen," he roared, not bothering to sound like Granny any more, "PULL ME UP, all three of you, and *quick*!"

So now all three girls worked together pulling up the wolf in the basket.

"When you reach the top," called out Seng, "the Magic Yum-Yum Nuts will make you better."

"Now be careful this time," said Old Greyface. "If the basket falls, I'll gobble you all up."

Up, up, up went the basket, nearer and nearer to the girls. Up, up, up came Old Greyface. He opened his mouth wide – the girls could see every tooth in his mouth – when, *flip!* They let go of the rope again and down fell the wolf – WHAM! and this time he was dead.

When Mum came home in the morning, you can be sure they had a tale and a half to tell her.

Grandmother's Donkey

by JOAN SMITH
illustrated by GUNVOR EDWARDS

"I'm a wise old bird," Grandmother was fond of saying, though that was not how Spiro would have described her.

It was nothing to do with riding the donkey; every woman on the island rode sideways on a donkey to town when she went there to sell her herbs. But Grandmother's was the only *lively* donkey; the only one which danced like a wild horse. When other donkeys were lazy, Athena would prance in circles and flick her back legs up in the air. She loved it when Grandmother fell off. Another donkey might refuse to walk in the heat, but Athena liked to gallop under the hot sun. A galloping donkey was a rare sight in those parts.

Grandmother loved Athena, and encouraged her wild ways with shouts, and she would flap her full, black skirts against the animal's ears. Every ride was a game.

Monday was a day when the donkey won. Grandmother, breathless, blinked up at the donkey as she sat on the ground among the olive trees, and Athena looked down at Grandmother. They seemed to be laughing together.

"Are you all right?" asked Spiro, running up to her. He shook her black skirts, covered now in pale dust from the earth of the olive grove.

"One to me; two to Athena," said Grandmother, "and I had begun to think she was slowing down." Gently she stroked the long, grey ears. "When her eyes shine like wet tar, you can tell she is pleased."

As Spiro and Grandmother walked up the hill to the taverna where Spiro lived with his parents, Grandmother shouted down to Athena, "I know you're scheming what to do next. Well, I can scheme better than a wayward donkey."

Mother had seen Grandmother fall off Athena once more, and she was not pleased when they walked into the kitchen. "You should give up that donkey," she scolded. "You'll break your leg bone one of these days."

Anxiously, she sliced peppers and onions into rings, salads for the visitors who would come to eat at the taverna that evening. She added, "Your Cousin Anna gave up her donkey five years back."

Grandmother pretended to laugh. "So now she rides a scooter. A *scooter*."

"I'm not suggesting that you do that," said Mother quickly. "Not for one moment. But you should stop riding Athena." To change the subject, Grandmother made a great show of chasing a stray cat out of the kitchen; a scraggy, grey creature that had been homeless for so long that it was quite wild. There were always cats round the taverna, hoping to find scraps of food.

"Don't do that," said Spiro. "She's beginning to get tame. She would be really friendly if I were allowed to feed her."

"I've told you, Spiro," said Mother gently, "that we can't have cats in the taverna. The visitors would not come to eat our food if they thought cats had been licking the plates. And the summer visitors to the island are our living."

"Just one cat," said Spiro. "Just one, to play with, and to talk to." Sometimes he felt lonely. The village was so small there was no one of his own age in it. His school friends were in the next village, too far away to see often in the summer.

Everyone else had someone to talk to; Mother and Father had each other, and all the visitors as well. Grandmother had Athena. He had no one special to whom he could tell his thoughts. Grandmother, who may not have been as wise as she believed, was nevertheless understanding and kind. More than that, she liked to interfere.

"Let the boy have a pet," said Grandmother.

"It's not possible," said Mother patiently, "in a taverna."

There was a sound coming up the valley, disturbing the peace of the late afternoon, and the dust of the roads. With a snort, Cousin Anna arrived at Grandmother's house on her scooter. Spiro could see her through the settling dust down the hill as she clambered off the machine.

Grandmother set off back down the hill, in vain trying to straighten her black head scarf as she went. Spiro sighed. Grandmother had Athena *and* Cousin Anna to talk to.

Grandmother and Cousin Anna were sitting on either side of a little table under the vine in the courtyard, when Spiro went to see the goat. On the table, an oil lamp gave a circle of friendly, yellow light. With their heads close together, they talked endlessly, neither listening much to the other. Sometimes they laughed loudly, like braying donkeys, and at other times they shouted. In one happy moment, Grandmother clouted Cousin Anna with a bunch of tiny green grapes which she had pulled off the vine above her. Cousin Anna sat laughing, with tears and grape juice running together down her cheeks.

"Now I visit all over the island," said Cousin Anna, touching her black head scarf tied smartly at the back of her neck. It was always in place. Grandmother's scarf, knotted under her chin, was still askew.

"And what is the use of that?" demanded Grandmother. "You go too fast to see anything, and always in a dust cloud."

Cousin Anna smiled knowingly, and got up to go. "Good night, Spiro," she called, seeing him walking back up the hill.

"Where have you been?" asked Grandmother.

"I went to see if the goat would be my friend."

"And would he?"

"He smells too much to be a friend to anyone except another goat."

Long after the sound of Cousin Anna's machine had died away, Grandmother sat in the dark and thought. As the owls in the olive trees called to each other, she decided what she must do.

The next day, the family were in for a surprise. Grandmother went to the olive grove where Athena lived. Usually the donkey would kick the trees and bite the bark; once she had leaned on the fence until it fell down. Today, she was staring dreamily at only a dandelion.

Grandmother explained her plan, and Athena seemed to talk back to her. Spiro wondered if they *really* could understand one another.

When she had finished talking to the donkey, Grandmother went up to the taverna; she had scarcely noticed how subdued Athena looked.

"Now, about that donkey," began Mother.

"I've made up my mind," said Father, ready to be really firm, well, fairly firm, with Grandmother.

"I will not be riding the donkey just now," said Grandmother meekly.

"Oh," said Mother, surprised.

"Ah," said Father, relieved.

"On one condition," added Grandmother. "That Spiro can have a pet of his own. One of those cats."

Father and Mother considered this carefully. It was worth almost anything if Grandmother would give up riding the lively donkey. She surely would break a leg otherwise.

"I don't see how we *can* have a cat," said Mother at last. It was strange, but on that island no one kept a dog for a pet. A dog ate too much, while a cat could live on scraps. And it was far too hot to keep a rabbit, or any small animal, in a cage.

"Hmmph," said Grandmother and bounced back down the hill. To Spiro's surprise, she did not go straight to Athena.

"She's up to something," said Mother.

Grandmother took her basket of herbs to town on the local bus, and Spiro went with her. "Thanks for trying," he said.

"I don't give up that easily," she replied.

When they had been to the market, and were waiting for the return bus, Grandmother suddenly shouted, "Look. There is Cousin Anna on her machine."

The thin, black figure sat amid the traffic, waiting for the green light, hunched up on the scooter like a cat watching a bird. The lights changed; the traffic came slowly to life. Cousin Anna shot out her right arm, straight and bossy; and turned sharp left.

The bus behind her braked, shuddering. Tyres yelped. Cousin Anna drove confidently away.

Catching sight of Spiro and Grandmother, she windmilled an arm round and round her head, steering with only one hand.

"Show off," said Grandmother, and turned her back. But when Spiro spoke to her on the bus, she did not even reply, she was so deep in thought.

* * *

"Was Grandmother quite well in the town?" asked Mother.

A cloud of white dust and the sound of the scooter told them that Cousin Anna had arrived once more to see Grandmother.

"She was the same as always," said Spiro. "A bit noisy."

"I think I should go and see her," said Mother, and went with Spiro down the hill. Strangely, the old ladies were not sitting as usual in the shady part of the courtyard. Spiro heard the sound of the scooter engine revving up again.

"Cousin Anna did not stay long," said Mother.

Walking round the corner of the house, they were almost knocked to the ground. The scooter shot past in front of them.

Grandmother was clinging to the handlebars with white fists, head thrown back by the speed of the

start. Both legs stuck out in front like the horns of a charging bull, her feet having lost their hold. Her skirt, knotted up round the waist for safety, did nothing to improve the sight.

Although flustered, Grandmother had the sense to steer round the earth track, instead of plunging down into the olive groves, and bouncing over the knotted roots. The lanky cats scattered before her, the chickens screeched with indignation. It was some time before she discovered how the brakes worked.

Grandmother and scooter scrunched to a halt, then still sitting astride the machine, she walked it backwards until she came level with the family, who had been watching open mouthed.

"Did you see how fast it went?" she said. "Athena is so slow beside a scooter."

Mother put her hand on Grandmother's arm. "The donkey was worry enough for me, but a scooter is out of the question at your age."

"You should try riding it," said Grandmother, not listening. "And so much easier to steer than Athena. I shall buy a scooter of my own with the herb money."

Spiro closed his eyes at the thought, and leaned back against the vine. The scooter was worse than a lively donkey. There *could* be nothing worse than Grandmother loose on the narrow, dusty roads, scattering people and goats and buses in all directions as she drove round the island.

"I'll give you lessons in riding it," offered Cousin Anna.

"Lessons?" said Grandmother. "*I* don't need lessons. Not at my age."

"What are we going to do?" moaned Mother, sitting down because she felt so weak.

Grandmother heaved herself off the scooter, and came to stand over her. "Of course, I would do

anything if you would let young Spiro try to tame one of the cats he's after. I'd even give up riding the scooter."

"Very well," said Mother. "Very well. Spiro, you can try to tame one of the cats. Just one, and you can train it to stay out of my kitchen."

Grandmother smiled, and looked fondly up the hill towards where Athena stood quietly in the shade, her eyes dulled through having no wild gallops with Grandmother.

"Poor donkey. You're missing our jolly rides," said Grandmother. "You must wait until Spiro has his cat. People can change their minds. But then, we can go galloping into town together once more."

Spiro had planned the taming programme. The key to it was food.

He had chosen the grey cat; she was the smallest, and thin as an empty bag. The name Willow, which he had always planned for the pet he would one day have, suited her perfectly.

83

Each night, when the plates of the visitors were cleared, Spiro would save the meat scraps in an old, chipped dish. Not that there was ever much left of Mother's cooking.

Then he would wait until he saw the grey cat, alone without the other strays, and put down the supper for her.

After a few meals she began to expect him, and came to the door the same time every night to wait.

"I'm making good progress," he told Grandmother. "She knows me already."

"I should take your time," said Grandmother, "because she looks very wild to me."

The next evening, he gently touched the top of the small, grey head. "You're going to be a house cat," he whispered.

But the cat had never before been touched by a human, unless she counted being kicked out of the kitchen by Father. She backed away, hissing.

"Willow," he said gently, hoping she would soon grow to fit the lovely name. "Don't be frightened, Willow. When you're a house cat you will have a warm bed for the winter; you'll never need to huddle between the tree roots to get out of the wind again."

Willow stared at him with cold, green eyes and ran off.

It was two weeks before the cat got used to the touch of his hand, and no longer hissed. But she

stood tense and ready for escape whenever he stroked her head. She never seemed to want to know her name; never even twitched an ear when he called her Willow.

It was on a particularly hot morning that Spiro saw Willow coming to find him early in the day. This he took as a friendly sign. He looked into her face and tried to catch a glimmer of love, but her eyes were hard and greedy.

Mother was watching him from the kitchen window. She smiled gently when he came in. "She has been unloved for so long, ever since she was a kitten," said Mother, "that it is hard for her to know how to love. It may be she will never know."

"She will change," said Spiro. "She's *got* to."

"And I have got to ride Athena again soon," said Grandmother. "She is growing so fat and miserable without our gallops. She stands down there among the olive trees, staring into space. She's lost all her spirit."

"Are you sure that's her problem?" asked Mother.

"Of course," said Grandmother, lifting up the lids of the cooking pots to see what there would be to eat later. "I'm off to talk to Athena now. She needs perking up." And Grandmother set off down the hill.

Spiro went outside with the dish holding a few scraps of raw mince. Willow was still waiting for him.

He stroked her head before he gave her the plate; she stared past him at the food.

Then gently, very gently, he picked her up.

Spiro felt as if he had been struck by lightning.

The cat was terrified; she thought she was caught in a trap and she sunk her teeth into his finger. She scratched at his face with her claws; she hissed and she growled like a dog.

Spiro dropped the cat and, despite himself, screamed out loud.

Father came running out of the kitchen where he had been cleaning the charcoal grills ready for the evening. He saw at once what had happened.

"To the town," he said, taking Spiro's hand and

pulling him towards the old truck. "You must see a doctor. Those cats are full of germs."

It was not until he was on his way back, hand bandaged, leg still aching from an injection, and face sticky with thick, yellow ointment, that Spiro cried.

It was not because of the pain, or because he had been frightened at the time that the tears ran down his face, avoiding the sticky ointment like cold water over a greasy plate. It was because he knew now that he could never tell that little animal his thoughts, for there is no love in a stray cat gone wild. It had all been only a dream.

He felt empty, as if he had lost his pocket money. It can really hurt to lose a dream.

As they drove past Grandmother's house, she ran out into the white, dusty road, flapping her arms up and down like a crow about to take off from the ground.

"Come," she shouted, "come at once," and she set off at a trot up to the olive grove.

"Better see what the old lady is up to," said Father. He knew there would be no peace until Grandmother got their attention.

Grandmother turned round to check that they were following her.

"Cats," she shouted. "Look what cats do for you, Spiro." Mother had already told her what had happened.

Father shook his head warningly. Spiro did not need Grandmother's opinion of cats this morning.

The old lady came to a stop and took Spiro's hand,

the unbitten one luckily. "We can do better than a bad tempered little cat," she said, quieter now, for she was out of breath. "Look at *that*."

Athena stood beneath the olive tree, gentle and proud, her eyes gleaming like wet tar.

Beside her stood the foal, on graceless, unsteady legs, its coat pathetically harsh for a baby animal, and so dark round the ears that the fur looked damp.

"I've never seen one so new," whispered Spiro, "nor so beautiful."

"And of course," said Grandmother, "she will be your own. She will be your very own donkey."

"So that was why Athena was so quiet," said Father. "And how lucky that you had not been making her gallop about the island."

"I'm a wise old bird," said Grandmother.

"Did you *know* she would have a foal?" asked Spiro.

But Grandmother preferred not to answer. "What will you call your new pet?" she asked.

"She really *is* Willow," said Spiro, and as the little animal nuzzled closer to her mother, he could see there was love already within her.

When the foal was older, Grandmother took to riding Athena again; but motherhood had changed

the donkey. She never bucked and she never galloped. She no longer danced, and she never once tossed Grandmother off her back. Mother stopped worrying because Grandmother rode slowly along the white, dusty roads on Athena, exactly like every other old lady taking her herbs to the town to sell.

But Willow grew up to be lively, as lively as her mother had once been. She often carried Spiro to the next village to see his friends; but best of all, she listened to his thoughts, and sometimes she told Spiro her own in return.

Puddle

by DICK KING-SMITH
illustrated by DAVID PARKINS

Sophie's birthday was on the twenty-fifth of December. Sophie was rather proud of this fact. Ages and ages ago, when she was only four, Sophie had said to her twin brothers Matthew and Mark, "I bet I'm the only girl who was ever born on Christmas Day."

"Course you're not," they said.

"Well, who else was then?" Sophie said. "Go on, tell me."

The twins looked at one another.

"I know!" said Matthew.

"I know what you're going to say!" said Mark.

"Jesus!" they cried.

Sophie looked scornful.

"Funny sort of girl," she said.

She plodded off to ask her mother and father, but they said that thousands of babies were born every day of the year, including Christmas Day.

"So there must be lots of other little girls who share your birthday," her mother said.

"I bet I'm the only one who's going to be a lady farmer," said Sophie.

"Well, that narrows it down a bit," said her father, "but I expect there are quite a number who share your ambition."

"What's an ambition?"

"Something you are determined to do."

Sophie, though small, was very determined, and she was not going to lose this argument.

"I bet," she said, "that I'm the only girl in the world who was born on Christmas Day and is going to be a lady farmer and is going to have a cow called Blossom and two hens called April and May and a pony called Shorty and a pig called Measles."

"Now there," they said, "you may be right."

All that was two years before. Sophie was six now, and the twins were eight – Matthew, as he always would be, ten minutes older than Mark.

Sophie was as determined as ever to be a lady farmer one day. For two years she had been saving up for this. On the side of her piggy bank was stuck a notice. Originally it had said:

Farm munny
thank you
Sophie

But since going to school, Sophie's spelling had improved, and now it read:

Farm monney
thank you
Sophie

At one time there had been ten pounds and ten pence in the piggy bank, but Sophie had spent three pounds of this on a collar and lead for one of her pets. These were a black cat called Tomboy, a white rabbit

called Beano, and a puppy, as yet without a name.
Strictly speaking, the puppy belonged to all the
family, but already Sophie thought of it as her own.

It had arrived this very day, her sixth birthday, the seventh Christmas Day of her life.

In fact Sophie had last used the collar and lead for Beano, so that he could exercise on the lawn, the loop of the lead dropped over a stake around which he grazed in a circle.

"The puppy can have the rabbit's collar and lead now, can't he?" Sophie's mother said that evening.

"No," said Sophie.

"Beano doesn't need them," said Sophie's father. "He's in his nice warm hutch for the winter. And in the summer you can always tether him with a bit of string."

"No," said Sophie.

"Why not?" they said.

"Because I bought them with my farm money. They're mine. And you said the puppy belongs to all of us. So I'll sell you all the collar and lead. You can all pay me for them."

"Not me," said Mark.

"Nor me," said Matthew.

"How much?" said Sophie's father.

Sophie rubbed the tip of her nose, a sure sign that she was thinking deeply.

"To you lot – three pounds, fifty pence," she said.

"How much did you pay for them in the first place?" her mother asked.

Sophie did not approve of telling lies.

"Three pounds," she said.

"You're asking more than when they were new!"

"Take it or leave it," said Sophie.

Her father took his pipe out of his mouth to give an admiring whistle.

"Quite the businesswoman," he said. "I can just see you at the market. You'll drive a hard bargain."

"I shan't," said Sophie. "I shall drive a Land Rover."

She sat on the floor beside the Christmas tree, the new puppy in her lap. He was a little terrier, white except for a black patch over his right eye.

"You haven't got a name, my dear," she said.

"We could call him Pirate," her father said.

"Why?"

"Because he's got a black patch over one eye."

"Or just Patch?" said Sophie's mother.

"Call him Mark," said Matthew.

"Or Matthew," said Mark, and they both giggled.

"You know what you are," said Sophie.

"Yes," they said, for they knew only too well what an angry Sophie always called them. "We're mowldy, stupid and assive!" they chanted, and they rolled about, laughing.

"You're ingerant, you are," said Sophie.

"Ignorant, you mean," they said.

"That too," Sophie said.

She put the puppy down and stood up and plodded off, shoulders hunched, the picture of disapproval.

"Come on now, Sophie," said her mother. "You choose a name."

"After all, it was you who liked this puppy best," her father said. "Andrew's dad told me."

Sophie's friend Andrew was a farmer's son, and their terrier Lucy was the mother of the nameless puppy.

Sophie turned around.

"Can we call him whatever I choose?" she said.

"If you like."

"Promise?"

"Oh, all right."

At that moment the puppy plodded off into a corner of the room. Here it squatted down and did a little pool on the carpet.

"Look at that!" cried the twins.

Sophie rubbed the tip of her nose.

"That's it," she said.

"What's what?" said her parents.

"What he's done. It's given me an idea for a name."

"What?" said everybody.

"Puddle," said Sophie. "Let's call him Puddle."

"Sophie!" said her mother.

"Ugh!" said her brothers.

"Give a dog a bad name," said her father.

"You promised," said Sophie.

So Puddle he was.

Taking the Cat's Way Home

by JAN MARK
illustrated by PAUL HOWARD

Jane's cat was called Furlong.

People said, "What a strange name for a cat," until they saw him. Then they understood. Furlong had a face and a tail, two ears and four feet. The rest was fur. You could hardly see his legs.

Kind people said, "What a fine cat." Rude people said, "That's not a cat, it's a feather duster."

William, at school, said, "That's not a cat, it's a loo brush," but that was not the worst thing he did.

Andrea never said things like that, because she liked Jane and she loved Furlong.

Andrea lived next door. She was one year older than Jane, so they were not in the same class at school, but they were friends.

"I can remember when you were born," Andrea said to Jane. This was not true, but she said it sometimes so that Jane would remember that Andrea was much older. Jane could not say that she remembered when Andrea was born. Even Furlong was older than Jane.

Every day Jane and Andrea walked to school together, on their own, because there were no roads to cross and lots of other people were going to school as well.

Jane's mother said to her, "Don't step in the road. Don't talk to strangers. Never let anyone give you a lift." She said it every day as Jane went down the path.

Then Andrea came out of her house and they walked together along the street, every day. Every day, Furlong went with them.

First of all he ran in front, and when he got to the corner he sat and waited for them. When they turned the corner, he ran to catch them up and walked beside them.

When they turned the last corner, Furlong ran on ahead and sat by the school gate until they got there too. Jane and Andrea stroked him and said goodbye.

Then they went in to school and Furlong walked home by himself. Jane thought he walked back the way they had come, but he did not. He had his own way home.

Everyone knew Furlong, all the people in Jane's class and all the people in Andrea's class. The teachers knew Furlong. So did Mrs Giles, the caretaker, and the lollipop lady. Mrs Kumari, the school secretary, knew Furlong because one wet morning he put his muddy paws on her new pink skirt. Jane was afraid she would be cross, but Furlong smiled in his fur and purred, and Mrs Kumari forgave him.

Everyone knew Furlong except William.

William was new.

One morning Jane and Andrea were saying
goodbye to Furlong when a new dad and a new boy
came along the street.

"What a fine cat," the new dad said. This was the
proper thing to say to Furlong, but
the boy just glared.

Jane looked at the boy and
the boy looked at Jane. He
put out his tongue and
made his eyes go funny.

When Jane went into her classroom the new boy was there with Mr Singh. Jane liked Mr Singh because he was kind and he had lovely whiskers, like Furlong.

"This is William," Mr Singh said. "He is going to be in our class. Who has an empty space at their table?"

Jane sat with Matthew and Habib and Alison.

There were two empty spaces at their table. "Don't put up your hand," Jane said to Alison.

She remembered the face that William had made when he saw Furlong. "We don't want him here."

But Matthew and Habib put up their hands and jumped up and down, so Mr Singh sent William to sit on one of the empty chairs.

He sat down opposite Jane and made his eyes go funny again. Then he kicked her, under the table.

At break time William went off with Matthew and Habib and they all stood together under a tree and whispered.

When it was time to go in again, Jane looked at William's chair and said to Alison, "Will you change places with me?"

"No, I won't," Alison said. "I don't want him making funny eyes at me."

When everyone had come indoors, Mr Singh said, "Now, get out your News books."

He gave William a book to write his News in.

William wrote, "My name is William."

He looked at Jane. Then he wrote, "I do not like cats," and turned his book round so that Jane could see what he had written.

Jane wrote, "There is a new boy at our table. He does not like cats. I do not like him."

Habib leaned over and said, "Why don't you find another table to sit at?"

"Yes," said Matthew. "We don't want any girls on this table, do we?"

They had never said anything like that before.

Next morning Jane said to Mum, "I don't want to go to school today."

"Do you feel poorly?" Mum asked.

"There's a new boy at school," Jane said. "He doesn't like cats."

"Lots of people don't like cats," Mum said. "You will have to get used to that."

"He doesn't like me, either," Jane said, but she still had to go to school.

She walked down the road with Andrea and Furlong. Furlong ran ahead, and sat and waited, and walked behind, and then overtook them and ran to the school, just as he always did.

People stopped and said hello to Furlong, and Furlong purred and waved his feathery tail.

Then William came along, without his dad. He did not say hello to Furlong. He leaned down and said "Sssss!" very loudly, and Furlong jumped away. No one had ever said that to him before, not even Mrs Kumari when he put mud on her skirt.

William said "Sssss!" again, and Furlong was frightened. He jumped on to the wall of the house by the school and his fur stood on end because he was angry.

"Leave my cat alone," Jane said.

Andrea said, "If you do that again I'll tell Mr Singh, and he will make you stand in the corridor."

"That's not a cat," said William. "That is a loo brush." Then he picked up a stone and threw it.

The stone did not hit Furlong but it scared him. He jumped on to the top of the wall and ran away, under the trees.

"I hate you!" Jane shouted, and hit William. William hit Jane, and Andrea ran inside to fetch Mr Singh.

"I can't have you fighting," Mr Singh said when he came out.

"She hit me first," William yelled.

"He threw a stone at Furlong," said Jane.

"Go inside at once," Mr Singh said. He was angry. Even his whiskers looked angry.

When they got to the classroom he said, "William, you are not to throw stones at *anything*. Go and sit down." William sat down and kicked Alison under the table.

"Now, Jane, stop crying," said Mr Singh. "You ought not to have hit William, even if he did throw a stone."

"But Furlong was frightened," Jane said. "He ran away. He'll get lost."

"I don't suppose he will," Mr Singh said. "He's a

grown-up cat and he knows his way about. Which way did he run?"

"He went along the wall by the school field," Jane said.

"Well, then, he was going the right way," said Mr Singh. "You live in Kemp Street, don't you? Cats have their own way of getting around. They don't have to walk in the street, like us."

Jane went to her table.

"Tell-tale. Tell-tale," William hissed.

"Tell-tale," said Matthew and Habib.

"I'll get you tonight," William said. "After school, I'll get you."

After school William's dad came to meet him.

"I'll get you tomorrow, then," said William.

Jane and Andrea ran all the way home and when they got there Furlong was sitting in the garden, washing his toes. Mr Singh was right. Cats have their own way home.

When Andrea and Jane and Furlong walked to school next day, William was waiting at the gate.

As soon as Furlong saw William, he jumped on to the wall. William did not even have time to say "Sssss!"

"Loo brush!" William shouted instead. Furlong turned round and ran away along the wall beside the school field.

"I don't care," Jane said loudly. "Cats have their own way home."

"Tell-tale," William said. "I'll get you after school."

"I'll get you after school," William said, at break.

116

"I'll get you after school," William said, at lunch time.

"William's going to get you at home time," said Matthew and Habib at afternoon break.

At home time Mr Singh told them to go. William went out quickly with Matthew and Habib, to lie in wait for Jane.

Jane stood at the gate with Andrea. William's dad was not there today, but they could see William's head poking round the corner, at the end of the road. When William saw Jane and Andrea, he hid.

"He's going to get us," Jane said.

"No he isn't," Andrea said. "We won't go home that way. We'll go home the way Furlong goes."

She climbed on to the wall of the house by the school. It went up like steps until it was as high as the wall by the school field.

"Quickly," Andrea said. "Here comes William."

Jane climbed on to the wall, walked up the steps and followed Andrea.

William and Matthew and Habib were already running down the street.

Andrea began to run and Jane ran behind her, along the wall. Then they stopped.

"Did they see us?" Andrea said.

"Where are you?" William shouted, in the street.

They could not see him and he could not see them.

"I can see you!" William yelled.

"He can't," Andrea said. "He thinks we're hiding by the gate. Come on."

"It's a long way to the ground," Jane said.

"Don't look down," Andrea said. "Walk slowly. We need not hurry now. Pretend you are walking on a tightrope."

Jane did not think that this would help.

"I know where you are! I'll get you," William shouted, far away.

Jane thought how silly he must look, and she felt better.

On one side of the wall was the school field. Mrs Giles was pushing a machine up and down, making

white lines on the grass for sports day. She did not see Andrea and Jane.

On the other side of the wall was a row of back gardens. They passed a garden full of roses and a garden full of rubbish. Things looked different from the top of the wall. This is what birds see, thought Jane. This is what Furlong sees.

Next they came to a garden with an apple tree at the end of it. Jane knew that tree. It hung over the field and in autumn people picked up the apples that fell from it.

Now the apples were small and green, Jane and Andrea had to step carefully over the branches.

Then they met a white cat sitting on the wall. It would not move. They had to step over the cat, too.

In the next garden was a prickly bush. It scratched their legs and Jane was afraid that they would fall into it, but they got past the prickly bush. In the garden after that, two people were sitting in deckchairs. One of them turned round and shouted, "Oi! What are you doing up there? Get down at once!"

"Run!" said Andrea, and they ran for seven whole gardens, over branches and through prickly bushes, along the wall.

At last they came to the end of the school field.

"We must turn left here," Andrea said. Now they were on the wall that ran along the end of the school field. There were no trees in these gardens and they could walk quickly.

Then Jane said, "Look."

Mrs Giles was not in the field any more, but over by the school was William. Matthew and Habib had got bored and gone home, but William began to run. Far away William shouted, "Now I'm going to get you!"

"He's seen us," Andrea said. "Quick. When we get to the next garden, turn right. There's a big tree to hide in."

It was a very big tree with very big leaves. It stood in a corner and four walls met under it, like a crossroads.

"This way," Andrea said, and they ran along a wide wall, out of the tree.

"Turn left," Andrea said. "Turn right. Turn right again."

They stopped running and looked round. They could not see the tree, or the school field, but they could see William.

Now William was on the wall as well, but he was going the wrong way.

They stood quite still until he was out of sight.

He was still shouting, "I can see you!"

"We're safe," said Andrea.

"We're lost," said Jane.

They stared all round. Jane was right. The gardens

looked different from the top of the wall, but the houses all looked the same.

"Our house has a window in the roof," Andrea said.

"My house has a creeper growing up it," Jane said.

They looked and looked, but most of the houses had windows in their roofs, and a lot had creeper growing up them. They sat down on the wall and wondered what to do.

"Let's go back," Jane said, but they could still hear William shouting far away, and they did not know how to go back.

"Mum will be waiting. She'll be cross," Jane said, and she began to cry.

"Don't be a baby," Andrea said, but she knew that her mum would be worried too if they did not get home soon.

"There is a swing in our garden," Jane said, and they looked again. There were five gardens with swings in them.

"We've got a shed," said Andrea.

All the gardens had sheds.

126

"I wish we could find a policeman," Andrea said, but there were no policemen walking on the walls, only cats.

Jane watched the cats and then she had an idea. She stood up and shouted, "Furlong! Furlong!"

"Don't be silly," Andrea said.

"It's not silly," Jane said. "I have a special voice for Furlong. He always comes when I call." She shouted again. "Furlong! Furlong!"

They waited, and waited.

Nothing happened.

"Try once more," Andrea said, and Jane called again. "Furlong! Furlong!"

Then Andrea stood up and pointed.

"I see him."

Far away a ginger cat was running along the wall towards them, waving his feathery tail. He came closer and closer. It was Furlong.

He ran up to Jane and put his muddy paws on her skirt. Jane stroked him. "Good Furlong," she said. "Now, take us home."

Furlong knew the way. He ran along the wall and then sat down and waited for them to catch up with him.

He turned left and they followed him. He turned right and they ran behind. He jumped on to the roof of a shed at the end of the garden. There was a swing in the garden and a creeper was growing up the side of the house.

The house next door had a window in the roof.

Jane's mum was taking the washing off the line. When she saw Jane and Andrea on the wall she dropped all the washing.

"Where did you come from?" she said, and ran to help them climb down.

"We've been taking the cat's way home," Jane said.

Then they heard William's voice again, but William was not shouting now. Far away, William was running along the wall, and William was crying.

William called, "Mum! Mum! I'm lost! Dad, I'm lost!" William had no cat to show him the way home.

"Who is this?" said Jane's mum when William reached Jane's garden.

"It's a poor little boy who has got lost," Andrea said, loudly.

Jane's mum lifted William down from the wall and led him indoors.

"Tell me where you live," Jane's mum said, "and I will take you home."

She walked down the street with William and made him hold her hand.

Jane and Andrea stood at the gate and watched. They did not say anything, but they smiled.

And Furlong, in his long fur, smiled too.

Fox, Alligator and Rabbit

TRADITIONAL
illustrated by LOUISE VOCE

Once there was a fast, wide river. On one side stood a market and on the other a town. So to get to the market from the town, you had to cross the river. But – and this was a mighty big "but" – in the middle of the river was Alligator. Now alligators have got their own special way of letting you know they're around – they try and eat you.

One day, Fox and Rabbit wanted to cross the river to the market. Rabbit was working on some kind of a plan.

"Say, Fox," he says, "is it true you foxes are known for being just about the smartest, cleverest creatures around?"

"Yep," says Fox.

"Then hows about you taking me across the river?"

"Sure," says Fox, "I'll do it for some of those melons you got there."

"That's fine," says Rabbit.

"Then you just watch me, Rabbit," says Fox, "and you'll see how to lick this alligator thing, no trouble."

So Fox hightailed out into the river, and you can be sure he knows some things that no one else knows. He knows that Alligator likes his porridge so hot it'd burn your eyelashes to eat it. And another thing – Alligator is stupid. He is so stupid he's been known to think his tail was a fish and give himself a terrible bite. WHEEEEE, that hurt!

So Fox is swimming along and he meets Alligator. One more thing about Alligator, he may be stupid, but believe me, he *thinks* he's one smart guy.

Fox gives him something like this: "Say, Alligator,

if I can come home with you and have a bite or two to eat with you, would you let me across this river?"

And something else about Alligator. He just loves to give people some of his roasting hot porridge and then sit back and watch them burn their mouths out – HOWOWEEE!

So you know what Alligator says when Fox is seriously inviting himself round to Alligator's place… ? "Sure – but I'll cook – and it'll be porridge."

And Alligator can hardly stop himself laughing, thinking about Fox's tongue hitting that hot porridge.

As soon as they get to Alligator's place, Alligator starts cooking the porridge. About two hours later, it's ready and he pours it out into a big, big bowl to eat.

Fox takes his spoon down to the porridge real slow, he lifts it up to his mouth just as slow and then as soon as it hits his tongue he says, "Oooh no, this is much too cold for me, Alligator. Why not put it out in the sun to warm up, huh?"

Alligator loves that. Make it even hotter. Great idea. Then it'll be so hot, Fox won't even be able to bear looking at it. He won't be crossing the river today, thinks Alligator, and he puts the porridge out in the sun.

Two hours later he brings it back in.

"Try that, Fox," says Alligator. He can hardly wait for the screams.

Down goes the spoon real slow, up it comes just as slow and then as soon as it hits Fox's tongue, he says, "Oooh no, it's still too cold. Put it out in the sun for a while more."

So out goes the porridge again, for three hours more. This porridge is going to be awful hot, thinks Alligator. Even I might find it tough getting it down me.

After all this time, the porridge is stone cold.

"I'll give it a try now," says Fox. "I just hope it's hotted up some."

Down goes the spoon real slow, up it comes just as slow and as soon as it hits Fox's tongue he says, "Hey, Alligator, now we are really cooking on all four burners. This is what I call hot. Just give me that porridge." And Fox digs into that porridge like there's no tomorrow.

Believe me, Alligator is impressed. He's sitting there figuring and figuring about how Fox's mouth can take all that burning.

With Fox finished, Alligator says to him, "If you like it that much, Brother, why not have some more?"

"I sure would like to," says Fox, "but I've got business at the market today. I've got to stock up on porridge."

And now Alligator says, "OK. I'll let you get across. It's been a pleasure to see someone like my porridge so much."

"The pleasure's mine," says Fox, and off he swims.

And as he's swimming along, Fox is thinking of those melons Rabbit has promised him. But Alligator's sitting there eating the cold porridge and he's figuring and figuring: how come my porridge is so cold but his porridge was getting hotter? Now that's something I must ask that Fox.

So quick as a fish, Alligator swims after Fox and in two blinks of an eye he's up to him.

"Say, Fox, tell me this, how come your porridge was hotter than mine?"

Sheesh, thinks Fox, he's figured it out. I'd better get these legs moving.

"What's that you say?" says Fox.

"How come your porridge—"

"My what?" says Fox.

"Your porridge."

"My pocket?"

"No, your porridge."

"What about my porridge?"

"How come it was hotter than mine?"

But by now, Fox has made it to the other side, and has climbed out on to the bank.

"I'll tell you tomorrow," says Fox and he's off to the market.

When he gets there, what do you know – Rabbit's standing there waiting for him.

"OK, big boy," says Fox, "how come you got across?"

And Rabbit says, "You're not the only one with a bit of sense round here. What do you think I was doing while you were with Alligator?"

At that he slaps his sides and whoops with laughter.

Fox watches him for a while and then says, kind of slow and soft, "So tell me this, Rabbit, if you weren't watching me to see how I got across just then, how are you going to get back?"

Rabbit stops all his laughing right there and then.

Acknowledgements

"Joshua" from *Willa and Old Miss Annie*
Text © 1994 Berlie Doherty Illustrations © 1994, 1995 Kim Lewis

"Little Ivan" from *Under the Moon*
Text © 1993 Vivian French Illustrations © 1993 Chris Fisher

"Tod and the Desperate Search" from *Here Comes Tod!*
Text © 1992 Philippa Pearce Illustrations © 1992 Adriano Gon

"Old Greyface" from *Clever Cakes and Other Stories*
Text © 1991 Michael Rosen Illustrations © 1991 Caroline Holden

Grandmother's Donkey
Text © 1983 Joan Smith Illustrations © 1983 Gunvor Edwards

"Puddle" from *Sophie in the Saddle*
Text © 1993 Fox Busters Ltd Illustrations © 1993 David Parkins

Taking the Cat's Way Home
Text © 1994 Jan Mark Illustrations © 1994 Paul Howard

"Fox, Alligator and Rabbit" from *South and North, East and West*
Edited text © 1992 Michael Rosen Illustrations © 1992, 1995 Louise Voce